Praying Freedom

*Lenten Meditations to Engage Your
Mind and Free Your Soul*

VINITA HAMPTON WRIGHT

LOYOLA PRESS.
A JESUIT MINISTRY
Chicago

LOYOLA PRESS.
A JESUIT MINISTRY

3441 N. Ashland Avenue
Chicago, Illinois 60657
(800) 621-1008
www.loyolapress.com

Unless otherwise indicated, Scripture quotations contained herein are
from the *New Revised Standard Version Bible: Catholic Edition*, copyright
© 1993 and 1989 by the Division of Christian Education of the
National Council of the Churches of Christ in the U.S.A. Used by
permission. All rights reserved.

Scripture taken from *The Message*. Copyright © by Eugene H. Peterson,
1993, 1994, 1995. Used by permission of NavPress Publishing Group.

Cover art credit: Johnny Franzen/Media Bakery

Library of Congress Cataloging-in-Publication Data
Wright, Vinita Hampton, 1958-
  Praying freedom : Lenten meditations to engage your mind and free
your soul / Vinita Hampton Wright.
      p. cm.
  ISBN-13: 978-0-8294-3844-4
  ISBN-10: 0-8294-3844-0
1. Lent--Prayers and devotions. 2. Catholic Church--Prayers and
devotions. 3. Liberty--Biblical teaching. 4. Liberty--Religious
aspects--Christianity--Prayers and devotions. 5. Bible--Devotional use.
I. Title.
  BX2170.L4W75 2013
  242'.34--dc23
                                                    2012036816

Printed in the United States of America.
13 14 15 16 17 18 Bang 10 9 8 7 6 5 4 3 2 1

Contents

Freedom and Lent

Freedom is the ability to make wise choices in the midst of emotional turmoil.

Freedom is a stance toward life that opens you to possibility and cultivates a positive outlook.

Freedom removes interior constraints so that you can follow the best way.

Freedom means that you truly have a choice.

Freedom moves you to greater love.

Freedom brings peace and makes a way for contentment.

How free am I? How free are you? During Lent, we have the opportunity to focus on our spiritual health, and inevitably we discover how un-free we are. In the

Gospel of John (8:34), Jesus stated that people who sin are slaves to sin, and the apostle Paul used similar terms in Romans 6:16, speaking of our slavery to sin, which leads to death.

So freedom is an appropriate topic for our Lenten meditations. Our prayers during this season can help free us from damaging thought patterns, bad habits, and that nagging sense of shame or failure.

A few centuries ago, St. Ignatius of Loyola wrote what came to be known as the *Spiritual Exercises*. Some key principles of spiritual direction, as practiced today, are based on what Ignatius laid out in his Exercises. He understood how un-free people tend to be, even when they are doing their best to follow God and to live healthy, holy lives. Often we are not free because we're not fully aware of how habits of thought, emotion, and behavior have enslaved us. Sometimes we see our un-freedom but don't know how to move out of it into freedom. Ignatius knew that freedom requires self-awareness as well as prayer; imagination as well as good intention, and practical activity as well as belief.

This book of Lenten meditations does not use material directly from the Spiritual Exercises. However, I have designed the chapters to emphasize aspects of prayer that are standard in Ignatian practice. These prayer experiences are rooted in Scripture; they invite the imagination to play its part; they encourage personal conversation with God; they suggest specific actions to take; and they provide immediate practices of prayer. I hope that *Praying Freedom* enhances your journey into awareness, wisdom, rest, inspiration, and ongoing conversion. God's great dream for you is that you grow in freedom to discover your true self, to live an authentic faith, and to enjoy abundant life.

Using This Book

Praying Freedom: Lenten Meditations to Engage Your Mind and Free Your Soul is filled with various prayer exercises designed to help you focus on what it means to be spiritually free. This book is organized to cover six weeks—time enough to include the forty days of Lent. However, because it can be daunting to try to follow a daily course of prayer, the material is not divided into days. Instead, each week consists of four key segments so that any one segment can be used over one or two days. Or an entire chapter can be covered in one reading if you prefer to concentrate more material into one period of prayer. For instance, during Lent you may choose to set aside retreat time on the weekend in which to cover a chapter of *Praying Freedom*.

Each chapter includes an Old Testament reading, a psalm, a New Testament Epistle reading, and a Gospel reading. The goal is to follow the topic of freedom throughout the Scriptures.

The four segments of each chapter are as follows:

Here's the Idea introduces the topic and focuses on mental understanding of it.

Use Your Imagination is designed to stimulate your imagination and other "right-brain" ways of praying.

Practice Your Freedom helps you choose how to apply the ideas personally and specifically.

Do the Prayer helps you focus on prayer as experience.

Don't be surprised if you connect with one type of exercise more than others. Some people will relate easily to Here's the Idea; others will be helped more by imaginative work. You may gravitate toward the practical aspects of Practice Your Freedom or enjoy Do the Prayer more than other parts of the book. Pay attention to what attracts you—and also to what elicits resistance within you. Whether your reaction to a type of exercise or a specific prayer is positive or negative, it merits more attention.

If a particular prayer exercise is powerful for you, don't hesitate to go back to it and repeat it.

I encourage you to keep a journal as you use *Praying Freedom*. A journal provides plenty of space to expand the experience and reflect on it. Some space for taking notes is provided in this book.

Before You Pray

Before trying to pray, it helps to get quiet and prepare for attentiveness. Here's one exercise to help with that. If it works for you, use it throughout the book before any time of prayer.

First, get comfortable. Find a good place to sit where you won't be disturbed. If it helps you relax, get a cup of coffee or tea, or a tall glass of water. If you like to journal, have a fresh page ready.

Take some breaths. Here's a little formula for good, deep breathing:

- Inhale through the nose for four or five seconds.

- Hold the breath for six or seven seconds.

- Exhale through the mouth for seven to eight seconds.

- Repeat three or four times.

Close your eyes and imagine that you're looking down at yourself. What is your posture—tense? Tired? Expectant? Relaxed? Look at your face, and try to read what the expression is telling you.

In your mind, or in your journal, list the two or three big concerns of your day. That is, what's at the top of your mind right now? As you go down the list, give each of these concerns to God:

> I'm letting go of this right now.
>
> Please keep this concern in your care while I spend this time with you.
>
> I'll try not to take it back or worry about it during this time.

Tell God how you feel as you embark on this time of meditation, rest, and prayer. Ask for what you need. Perhaps pray an Our Father, a Hail Mary, or another traditional prayer as you begin.

1

Freedom Is Grounded in Truth

Then Jesus said to the Jews who had believed in him, "If you continue in my word, you are truly my disciples; and you will know the truth, and the truth will make you free."

—John 8:31–32

Here's the Idea: No Truth, No Freedom!

†

Who would ever have thought it possible—just when we thought things couldn't get worse, they did. What the drought didn't destroy, the floods have now swept away. What the tornadoes left, the gangbangers took. What the thieving Wall Street players left, the banks have foreclosed upon. Everything we try doesn't work—the evil is too deeply rooted in the way we do things. Our structures are broken, and our systems are dysfunctional. Even the environment and the animals suffer because of humanity's neglect, greed, and wickedness.

We should all be crying day and night in grief for how things are. We should grieve so much we can't eat or drink. Every one of us has to take a cold, hard look at how we have participated in this awful mess. In truth, we've brought most of it on ourselves.

—Joel 1; Vinita's adaptation for our time of the prophet
Joel's words

It's difficult to make a good decision when you don't have all the information. It's also difficult to move forward while trying to deny part of your reality. Jesus came from a tradition that was brutally honest; just read a bit from any of Israel's prophets to see how forcefully they spoke the truth. Jesus continued in this vein as he talked about what it really took to be people of God, to participate in the kingdom of God.

Jesus knew what John the Baptist knew before him and what the prophets knew before both of them: without truth, people cannot heal. If we ignore the root cause of our wounds, we will continue to be wounded, even if we heal some of the damage. We might fix what has been harmed. But if we continue doing what caused the harm in the first place, we will simply acquire (or inflict) new wounds because the core activity has not changed.

Lent is a good time to stop our activity long enough to look at it carefully, prayerfully, and to determine the specific truths of the situation. For example:

- Am I exhausted because the schedule of the past month went out of control—or am I exhausted because I keep taking on responsibilities that are not mine to take on?

- Do I keep butting heads with this coworker because she doesn't appreciate what I offer to the team—or have I misunderstood her perspective, her way of processing information, and her best strategies for getting things done?

- Am I failing at a simple habit of daily prayer because I'm lazy—or is there some resistance inside me that I need to deal with?

What are your thoughts, feelings, and impressions on this topic of truth-telling? Write in a journal, draw pictures, sing, or move physically if that will help your process.

_____

_____

_____

_____

_____

_____

_____

_____

_____

_____

_____

_____

_____

Use Your Imagination

✝

For freedom Christ has set us free. Stand firm, therefore, and do not submit again to a yoke of slavery.

—Galatians 5:1

A yoke was a wooden structure placed on the necks of teams of cattle or oxen so that they could pull carts or plows. When the animal was yoked, it could not determine its own movements but was at the mercy of its master.

Draw a picture of yourself. If you're not an artist, it can be a simple stick figure.

Now, draw a yoke across your neck and shoulders. This may represent whatever prevents you from determining your own actions. Everyone has a yoke, and some yokes are better or worse than others. For example, most of us have to go to work to earn a living; this isn't necessarily a bad yoke, but it does have an impact on how free we are to determine what we do and when. The idea is not to get rid of every yoke but to be honest about what the yoke is.

The yoke you draw might represent what keeps you from being free in the interior life. For instance, many people wear a yoke of anger, which guides their emotions into the same well-worn paths, day after day. For others, it might be anxiety or despair.

All around the picture of you and the yoke, write the words that give specific labels and descriptions to your yoke. Then circle words and phrases that represent yokes you need to be rid of. You will discover that, while some yokes are inescapable, others are a matter of choice, and you can choose not to wear those yokes any longer.

_____

_____

_____

_____

_____

_____

_____

_____

_____

_____

_____

_____

_____

_____

Practice Your Freedom

Consider this your week of truth-seeking. Try any or all of these exercises:

- When you are tempted to make an excuse, stop. If you threw away the excuse, what would you have to say?

- When someone asks how you are, really think about your answer. If the person asking is a friend and really wants to know, then give an honest answer. You may not be fine. You may be tired or frustrated. Or you may be better than fine—especially grateful for something or someone in your life. Whatever the case, tell the truth.

- Write out a simple prayer, which begins like this: "God, to be completely honest, this is how I feel about my life right now . . ."

Make some notes here about the action you plan to take this week.

_____

_____

_____

_____

_____

_____

_____

_____

_____

_____

_____

_____

_____

Do the Prayer

Psalm 139 is a heartfelt, honest, and intimate prayer between an individual and God. Try praying it as your own prayer. Repeat the phrases that are meaningful to you. Pray it silently or whispered or out loud. Allow these prayer thoughts to inspire your own. Notice how nothing is hidden; all is known—the truth is out!

✝

LORD, you have searched me and known me.
You know when I sit down and when I rise up;
   you discern my thoughts from far away.
You search out my path and my lying down,
   and are acquainted with all my ways.
Even before a word is on my tongue,
   O LORD, you know it completely.
You hem me in, behind and before,
   and lay your hand upon me.
Such knowledge is too wonderful for me;
   it is so high that I cannot attain it.

Where can I go from your spirit?
   Or where can I flee from your presence?
If I ascend to heaven, you are there;
   if I make my bed in Sheol, you are there.
If I take the wings of the morning

and settle at the farthest limits of the sea,
even there your hand shall lead me,
    and your right hand shall hold me fast.
If I say, "Surely the darkness shall cover me,
    and the light around me become night,"
even the darkness is not dark to you;
    the night is as bright as the day,
    for darkness is as light to you.

For it was you who formed my inward parts;
    you knit me together in my mother's womb.
I praise you, for I am fearfully and wonderfully made.
    Wonderful are your works;
that I know very well.
    My frame was not hidden from you,
when I was being made in secret,
    intricately woven in the depths of the earth.
Your eyes beheld my unformed substance.
In your book were written
    all the days that were formed for me,
    when none of them as yet existed.

. . .

Search me, O God, and know my heart;
    test me and know my thoughts.
See if there is any wicked way in me,
    and lead me in the way everlasting.

_____

_____

_____

_____

_____

_____

_____

_____

_____

_____

_____

_____

_____

_____

_____

_____

_____

_____

_____

_____

_____

_____

_____

_____

_____

_____

2

Freedom Grows with Faith

. . . let us also lay aside every weight and the sin that clings so closely, and let us run with perseverance the race that is set before us, looking to Jesus the pioneer and perfecter of our faith . . .

—Hebrews 12:1–2

Here's the Idea: Trust Leads to Freer Movement

✝

Is there anyone among you who, if your child asks for bread, will give a stone? . . . If you then, who are evil, know how to give good gifts to your children, how much more will your Father in heaven give good things to those who ask him!

—Matthew 7:9,11

You need to have a heart-to-heart with your supervisor at work. You have ideas about how to adjust a process so that projects will become more streamlined. You even have a plan to try and a list of resources you'll need. All you have to do is talk with your supervisor. Right now you're standing outside her office door.

If you have faith in your supervisor's goodwill, walking through that door won't be a difficult thing. If you trust her to listen to you, to be open to your suggestions, and to entrust you with responsibility, then you'll go right in, sit down, and have a good discussion.

However, if you don't have a lot of faith in your supervisor, the situation could play out quite differently. If you perceive her as egocentric, unwilling to hear others' ideas, or reluctant to trust your skills, then you won't be free to talk openly with her and share your ideas. In fact, if you don't have faith in your supervisor to be a good supervisor, chances are you won't even go through her door and try to have a conversation.

Faith—or trust—makes it possible for us to experience freedom. This is true for our relationships with other people, but it's also true for our relationship with God. If we trust God to care for us, to listen to our prayers and help us, then we will be freer to pray, freer to engage with life and explore possibilities.

But if we think that God is essentially a bigger, badder version of us—a grand judge waiting to catch us in a crime or a zealous parent trying constantly to improve us—we won't be too eager to walk through the door and sit down for a heart-to-heart. Our dreams and visions for a good life will wither before we even get started.

What are your thoughts, feelings, and impressions on this topic of trust and freedom? Write in a journal, draw pictures, sing, or move physically if that will help your process.

_____

_____

_____

_____

_____

_____

_____

_____

_____

_____

_____

_____

_____

_____

_____

_____

_____

_____

_____

_____

_____

_____

_____

Use Your Imagination

†

O dry bones, hear the word of the LORD. Thus says the Lord GOD to these bones: I will cause breath to enter you, and you shall live. I will lay sinews on you, and will cause flesh to come upon you, and cover you with skin, and put breath in you, and you shall live . . .

—Ezekiel 37:4–6

The prophet Ezekiel had a now-famous vision of dry bones being reconstituted into living people. This vision served as a vivid promise from God to the people of Israel, a promise that they would come to life again—that all the sin and trouble they had experienced could not stop God from living powerfully through them.

Close your eyes. Allow thoughts and images to move through your mind of all the damage in your life—damage caused by others and damage you've done to yourself.

Now imagine this: Whatever damage has been done to you—even your ultimate death—cannot stop God's love for you. If you can even begin to believe that God's love for you will transform every wrong step, every horrible memory, every statistic that goes against your success—if you can begin to have faith in God's powerful love, imagine how free you will be simply to do what you envision. This is faith that leads to freedom.

Imagine yourself as a skeleton of dry bones, lying in a desolate valley. Then the breath of God's love blows across you. You begin to be formed anew. Flesh appears on your bones. Dried-up organs come to life. Your eyes open, and your tongue begins to form words. You begin to feel yourself again—you are alive! You can move!

Allow your imagination to work with this scene. Then journal about the experience.

_____

_____

_____

_____

_____

_____

_____

_____

_____

_____

_____

_____

_____

Practice Your Freedom

This week, work on building your trust in God's help and care.

- In a given situation, act as if everything really will work out. Allow this to influence what you say to others and what you say to yourself.

- Recall at least one situation in which you felt that God was helping you. Try to recall it in detail, and then thank God for that care from the past.

- Do one thing that stretches you—a task that seems hard or an endeavor that's in line with your desires but that you can't do on your own. Ask for God's help—and then give it a try.

Make some notes here about the action you plan to take this week.

_____

_____

_____

_____

_____

_____

_____

_____

_____

_____

_____

_____

_____

Do the Prayer

Sometimes we must remind ourselves that God is worth trusting. The psalmist knew this. Often the Hebrew psalms were angry and questioning, but the people could cry out for justice and help because, at the root of it all, they trusted God. So this psalm, like various others, is a song about why we should trust God. Pray it silently or out loud. Pray it once or twenty times. Allow Scripture to reinforce in you the image of a loving God who longs to hear and answer your prayers.

✝

Praise the LORD!
Praise the LORD, O my soul!
I will praise the LORD as long as I live;
    I will sing praises to my God all my life long.
Do not put your trust in princes,
    in mortals, in whom there is no help.
When their breath departs, they return to the earth;
on that very day their plans perish.

Happy are those whose help is the God of Jacob,
    whose hope is in the LORD their God,
who made heaven and earth,

the sea, and all that is in them;
who keeps faith forever;
  who executes justice for the oppressed;
  who gives food to the hungry.

The LORD sets the prisoners free;
  the LORD opens the eyes of the blind.
The LORD lifts up those who are bowed down;
  the LORD loves the righteous.
The LORD watches over the strangers;
  he upholds the orphan and the widow,
  but the way of the wicked he brings to ruin.

The LORD will reign forever,
  your God, O Zion, for all generations.
Praise the Lord!

—Psalm 146:1–10

_____

_____

_____

_____

_____

_____

_____

_____

_____

_____

_____

_____

_____

_____

_____

_____

_____

_____

_____

_____

_____

_____

_____

_____

_____

_____

_____

3

Freedom Holds Life Lightly

Unless the LORD builds the house,
  those who build it labor in vain.
Unless the LORD guards the city,
  the guard keeps watch in vain.
It is in vain that you rise up early and go
      late to rest,
eating the bread of anxious toil;
  for he gives sleep to his beloved.

—Psalm 127:1–2

Here's the Idea: Freedom Is the Opposite of Grasping

†

Then he said to them all, "If any want to become my followers, let them deny themselves and take up their cross daily and follow me. For those who want to save their life will lose it, and those who lose their life for my sake will save it. What does it profit them if they gain the whole world, but lose or forfeit themselves?"

—Luke 9:23–25

Psalm 127, which opens this chapter, is a great reality check for the Type A personality. No matter what we do, our own labor will take us only so far. Ultimately, we depend on God's care and help. The psalmist says, speaking for God, "Get some sleep. Let go—you're not in control anyway."

We find a similar message in Luke 9, but Jesus is quite blunt and more directive. He says that the person whose focus in life is self-preservation will not survive. The psalmist was speaking of God's watching over the world; it's almost a comforting few verses. But Jesus puts the responsibility on every person to decide his or her approach to life. Anyone wanting to follow the way of Jesus cannot go through life grasping and striving. It's impossible to enjoy abundant life while making self-preservation a top priority. Jesus adds urgency to the psalmist's message: "Let go—or you'll end up losing everything."

Letting go can also be described as holding life lightly. When we hold life lightly, we are not clinging or grasping. Our fists are not clenched. Our energy is not focused upon acquiring and keeping. Whatever we hold lightly, we can still enjoy, but we no longer try to force our will upon it or possess it only for ourselves.

How many ways do we strive and cling and try to save ourselves? What exactly are we trying to hold or keep, or preserve?

- a satisfied image of self
- others' high opinion of our personality and contributions
- our position at the workplace

- an income level that, in our minds, is nonnegotiable
- a relationship we must make work
- children we want to make us look like a high-functioning family

A fail-safe way to identify ways in which we're grasping at life is to ask the simple question *What do I fear?* Usually, our fears correlate pretty directly with what we don't want to lose, what we want to hang onto, no matter what.

Jesus asks us to go about life quite differently. Rather than allowing fear to determine our plans and actions, we are to reorient ourselves to what we already have, which is God's presence always and everywhere.

What are your thoughts, feelings, and impressions on this topic of grasping? Write in a journal, draw pictures, sing, or move physically if that will help your process.

_____

_____

_____

_____

_____

_____

_____

_____

_____

_____

_____

_____

_____

_____

Use Your Imagination

✝

Then the LORD said to Moses, "I am going to rain bread from heaven for you, and each day the people shall go out and gather enough for that day. In that way I will test them, whether they will follow my instruction or not. On the sixth day, when they prepare what they bring in, it will be twice as much as they gather on other days." So Moses and Aaron said to all the Israelites, "In the evening you shall know that it was the LORD who brought you out of the land of Egypt, and in the morning you shall see the glory of the LORD, because he has heard your complaining against the LORD."

—Exodus 16:4–7

This morning, while you're having your breakfast, an elderly and distinguished-looking gentleman walks up and sits down across from you. You exchange looks, and without his saying anything, you know that this is Moses. Yes, *that* Moses, sitting across from you at breakfast. You say good morning, but then you just sit and wait for him to speak. He looks like the kind of person who has important things to say.

"The Lord sent me to you," he begins, "because you worry too much. We need to work on that."

"We do?"

"Yes. And here's what will happen—today, and tomorrow, and for quite a few days. Listen very carefully."

You stop eating, put down your cereal spoon, and wait.

"Each morning, you'll go outside and stand at the edge of the street that goes by your house. You'll notice that the street is shiny. That's because, scattered across it, all up and down the block, are gold coins."

"Gold?" Your heart rate goes up immediately. *Gold?*

"Yes. Gold coins, each worth $50. And you are to pick up the coins you'll need for the day's expenses."

"I get to pick up the gold coins?"

"Yes. But—listen, because this is important—you pick up only what you need for the day."

"How will I know what I need?"

"Count up meals, transportation costs, and if there's a bill due, you can count that, too."

Your mind is racing. "But what—what if I need the car repaired?"

"You can count that."

"What if the kids ask me if they can go to the movies?"

"If going to the movies is a good plan for the day, certainly—pick up the gold needed for movies."

Your head is swimming. This is too good to be true! But then you get worried, and you have to ask: "Um. Can I do this early in the morning? Before the neighbors might be up and see what I'm doing?"

"Oh, they'll be doing the same thing."

"They will? They'll be picking up gold off the street?"

"Yes. And they have the same instructions—to pick up only what they need for the day."

"Does this deal include things like mortgage payments?" You're looking for loopholes now. This really is too good to be true. There must be a catch.

"Yes. It includes your needs. Simple as that. However, because you and your neighbors will all be out there together, picking up gold, you'll need to help one another."

You feel a bit panicked. "What do you mean, help one another?"

"Each morning there will be enough gold in the street for each family's needs. But no more than that. Which means that if one family picks up too much gold, someone else must do without."

Moses sees the expression on your face and continues. "For example, you might be tempted to pick up enough gold coins to buy a new flat-screen TV for your patio. But Marjie, two doors down, must pay a medical bill."

"I see, I see," you say. Just when your imagination had begun to conjure a second car, a refurbished bathroom, season basketball tickets, and so forth.

"Is that a problem for you?" asks Moses, looking wise and very, very patient.

"Of course not. I mean, how could I complain? My needs are being taken care of. All I have to do is pick up coins—and use discretion."

"And pay attention to your neighbors' needs as well as your own," Moses says. "And have conversations with other people. And spend time together every day, helping one another gather what each person needs."

"You said this would go on for quite a while. Can you tell me exactly how many days this will happen?"

"No. And you don't need to concern yourself with that. Now, if you were allowed to stock up on gold coins—to tuck them away for the future—I can see why you would worry about how many days the gold will appear. But you can gather only what you need, each day, for as long as the gold arrives."

"This is supposed to help me stop worrying?"

Moses looks at you and smiles, sort of the way a grandfather smiles at a toddler who has just said something very silly but with all seriousness. "The worry will stop when the trust begins. So why don't you concentrate on what it feels like to trust, every morning, just for that day?"

What's your reaction to this little story? How do you feel about having all your needs provided for? When you discover that everyone else has been given the same gift, what is your first thought or emotion?

_____

_____

_____

_____

_____

_____

_____

_____

_____

_____

_____

_____

_____

Practice Your Freedom

Identify two areas in your life in which you tend to strive for control. For each area, answer these questions:

- Why is control so important to me in this situation or area?

- What would happen if, today, I relinquished the control I do have?

- What am I really afraid of—what's the worst that could happen?

Talk to Jesus about these issues. Be very frank about what worries you and why it's difficult to give up control.

Now, try to come up with a simple plan for loosening your grip. Be realistic—you want to take a step, that's all. Jesus' disciples were slow to understand most of what he taught them, and they progressed one step at a time, one day at a time. Your efforts probably won't be much different from theirs.

Example: I'm a wife and mother of three, the two older kids in their teens. It seems that I spend hours (and hours) every week getting them to help keep the house halfway clean and organized. I'm exhausted from the effort, but if I don't keep nagging people (including my husband, to be honest), the house will be in ruin. This issue has me anxious and irritated a large portion of the time; it would be nice to have a conversation with another family member without the "cleaning" issue taking over.

It won't help to just stop caring about having a clean house; after all, a clean house is a reasonable goal. But I need to loosen my grip and relinquish control. So I make a chart that clearly states what each person's responsibilities are. Before showing this to anyone, I look at it and revise it—relieving every person of some tasks and accepting that, at least for a while, these tasks may not get done regularly if at all. But I'm willing to let go of those tasks. Even if I do most of the chart-making, I involve my husband—otherwise I'm communicating that this is really my house, not ours. Then I present the chart, explain it, and put it where it's easy to see. We remind the kids that their allowance and other privileges will be contingent on their work getting done.

Then I don't say anything else. I relinquish my ideal of a clean house. I don't say anything when chores don't get done. I don't criticize how thoroughly or imperfectly people do their jobs. I do make adjustments to allowances or privileges or whatever incentives are involved, according to the work done. I make the adjustments, but I don't preach or scold.

I try this for a month. It takes daily prayer and the quieting of my own spirit to prevent explosions on my part. I'm tempted to make sarcastic remarks or to verbalize threats, but I've given up these tactics.

Does it "work"? Maybe it does, and maybe not. But how well it works is not the main point. The real issue is my willingness to stop nagging and grasping, to allow "my" home *not* to conform to my personal standards. The fact is, if I can't let go of this, then there are doubtless other, more crucial issues that I'm also trying to control. There are other relationships being damaged by my grasping.

Make some notes here about what action you plan to take this week to loosen your grip on one or two areas of your life.

_____

_____

_____

_____

_____

_____

_____

_____

_____

_____

_____

_____

_____

_____

_____

_____

_____

_____

_____

_____

_____

_____

Do the Prayer

†

For you were called to freedom, brothers and sisters; only do not use your freedom as an opportunity for self-indulgence, but through love become slaves to one another. For the whole law is summed up in a single commandment, "You shall love your neighbor as yourself." If, however, you bite and devour one another, take care that you are not consumed by one another.

—Galatians 5:13–15

Today, or during the next few days, have a conversation with God about how you are tempted to be self-indulgent and to use your freedom mainly to reach after what you want. Just be honest; nothing you pray will surprise God, and you need to say it for your own sake. You need to hear yourself describe how you use freedom wrongly sometimes. If you don't say it out loud, at least write it down and read it several times.

As you dwell on your weak points of self-indulgence and grasping, make up some one-sentence prayers such as "Please help me

recognize when I'm ignoring other people's needs" or
"Remind me to listen more than talk" or "Help me
ask myself at least once today: am I using my freedom
with love and wisdom?"

_____

_____

_____

_____

_____

_____

_____

_____

_____

_____

_____

_____

_____

_____

_____

_____

_____

_____

_____

_____

_____

_____

4

Freedom Opens Its Hands and Heart

Make me to know your ways, O LORD;
teach me your paths.
Lead me in your truth, and teach me,
for you are the God of my salvation;
for you I wait all day long.

—Psalm 25:4–5

Here's the Idea: God's Extravagance Waits for Our Openness

✝

Ho, everyone who thirsts, come to the waters; and you that have no money, come, buy and eat! Come, buy wine and milk without money and without price. Why do you spend your money for that which is not bread, and your labor for that which does not satisfy? Listen carefully to me, and eat what is good, and delight yourselves in rich food. Incline your ear, and come to me; listen, so that you may live. . . .

Seek the LORD while he may be found, call upon him while he is near; let the wicked forsake their way, and the unrighteous their thoughts; let them return to the LORD, that he may have mercy on them, and to our God, for he will abundantly pardon. For my thoughts are not your thoughts, nor are your ways my ways, says the LORD. For as the heavens are higher than the earth, so are my ways higher than your ways and my thoughts than your thoughts.

—Isaiah 55:1–3, 6–9

Whatever we receive from divine love, we receive absolutely free. There's nothing we have ever done, or might do now, or could ever do, to move God to love us any more than we are already loved.

We agree with such statements, and we say them and write them and teach them. But on a day-to-day basis, often we are still trying to be worthy, to somehow deserve favor or help or blessing. When something good happens, we are likely to respond—at least inwardly—with a blush of guilt because we've done nothing to merit such good fortune.

In other words, we are not free simply to receive gifts and enjoy them. In our mind-set, we are still too tied up in a system of reward and punishment. After all, society works that way most of the time. "Nothing is for free," is the message, or "you get exactly what you pay for." Particularly in U.S. culture, with our history of the pioneer spirit and self-reliance and hard work, we often don't have room, emotionally, for a life that is blessed through no effort of our own.

When Isaiah says, on God's behalf, "My ways are higher than your ways and my thoughts than your thoughts," he's emphasizing how God's ways transcend every human system. When we turn to God—through hope or repentance or gratitude—we are standing in a space that is wide open, unfathomable. God waits for our hearts to open up to the possibilities, even as our minds have no idea what those possibilities might be.

God says to us right now: "Come, drink! Eat! Enjoy! Open your heart . . ."

What are your thoughts, feelings, and impressions on this topic of openness? Write in a journal, draw pictures, sing, or move physically if that will help your process.

_____

_____

_____

_____

_____

_____

_____

_____

_____

_____

_____

_____

_____

Use Your Imagination

†

As he was setting out on a journey, a man ran up and knelt before him, and asked him, "Good Teacher, what must I do to inherit eternal life?" Jesus said to him, "Why do you call me good? No one is good but God alone. You know the commandments: 'You shall not murder; You shall not commit adultery; You shall not steal; You shall not bear false witness; You shall not defraud; Honor your father and mother.'" He said to him, "Teacher, I have kept all these since my youth." Jesus, looking at him, loved him and said, "You lack one thing; go, sell what you own, and give the money to the poor, and you will have treasure in heaven; then come, follow me." When he heard this, he was shocked and went away grieving, for he had many possessions.

—Mark 10:17–22

This passage is used often as a commentary on riches. But it speaks also to freedom or the lack of it. Jesus was rooting for this young man. The story states that Jesus loved him and was drawn to this man's questions and desire. And when the man asked the critical question "What do I do now?" Jesus gave an honest answer. He intuited what the young man was afraid to lose: his wealth and security. Jesus aimed at the one thing that prevented the man from being completely free.

Imagine this. Jesus is leading a retreat at your church. Of course you attend—it's Jesus! And when you approach him for a few private moments, he gives you his full attention. He looks at you with warmth; *he's rooting for you* and wants to see you have the abundant life of which he speaks.

He patiently listens as you tell him about your spiritual journey thus far—all the dips and turns, the moments of conversion, the struggles, the epiphanies. He follows every word; he really wants to know what's going on with you. He nods and smiles when you relate the many ways in which your life has stretched and grown, as you describe the various ministries you've been involved with. You can tell from his eyes that he's truly pleased with you. He's happy for your spiritual progress.

But then you pause, and you say, "You can see that I've been trying to follow your way for many years, and sometimes I've done better than others. I feel that I'm in a pretty good place right now. But since you're sitting right here with me today, I have to ask: What should I do next? You see all hearts and have infinite wisdom. What can I do now, that will please you most?"

Remember, Jesus doesn't want people who merely do as they're told. He doesn't want people who work, work, work and worry, worry, worry. He wants people to know joy and to laugh a lot. He wants them—he wants *you*—to be completely free to enjoy God's kingdom.

So, what do you think Jesus will say to you now? What "one thing" is preventing your freedom?

_____

_____

_____

_____

_____

_____

_____

_____

_____

_____

_____

_____

_____

Practice Your Freedom

The next time someone gives you a gift, say thank-you and then enjoy that gift thoroughly.

The next time a project or meeting goes well, say thank-you (to God, to other people involved, even to yourself).

Ask God for what you want—what you really want. Then say something like this: "That's what I want, but if there's something better that you know about but I don't, I'll take the better thing."

The next time someone offers help, accept it—and say thank-you.

Ask God to help you dig down to the true hunger and thirst within you.

Make some notes here about the action you plan to take this week.

_____

_____

_____

_____

_____

_____

_____

_____

_____

_____

_____

_____

_____

_____

Do the Prayer

✝

If you choose, you can keep the commandments,
    and to act faithfully is a matter of your own choice.
He has placed before you fire and water;
    stretch out your hand for whichever you choose.
Before each person are life and death,
    and whichever one chooses will be given.
For great is the wisdom of the Lord;
    he is mighty in power and sees everything;
his eyes are on those who fear him,
    and he knows every human action.
He has not commanded anyone to be wicked,
    and he has not given anyone permission to sin.

—Sirach 15:15–20

We are free to make choices. But we become free to make wise choices as we grow more open to God and recognize the meaning and consequences of our decisions.

Draw some pictures based on phrases and images in this passage. What does death look like? What does life look like? Ask the Holy Spirit to help you come up with images for fire and water, life and death—what those things are in your situation. Ask to see clearly what your choices are—today, this week or month, this year.

You might draw this prayer two or three times this week; it's likely that each time you draw it, different images will emerge.

_____

_____

_____

_____

_____

_____

_____

_____

_____

_____

_____

_____

_____

5

Freedom Brings Healing and Reconciliation

Now the Lord is the Spirit, and where the Spirit of the Lord is, there is freedom. And all of us, with unveiled faces, seeing the glory of the Lord as though reflected in a mirror, are being transformed into the same image from one degree of glory to another; for this comes from the Lord, the Spirit.

—2 Corinthians 3:17–18

Here's the Idea: When We're Free, We Can Receive Help

✝

Naaman, commander of the army of the king of Aram, was a great man and in high favor with his master, because by him the LORD had given victory to Aram. The man, though a mighty warrior, suffered from leprosy. Now the Arameans on one of their raids had taken a young girl captive from the land of Israel, and she served Naaman's wife. She said to her mistress, "If only my lord were with the prophet who is in Samaria! He would cure him of his leprosy." So Naaman went in and told his lord just what the girl from the land of Israel had said. And the king of Aram said, "Go then, and I will send along a letter to the king of Israel."

He went, taking with him ten talents of silver, six thousand shekels of gold, and ten sets of garments. He brought the letter to the king of Israel, which read, "When this letter reaches you, know that I have sent to you my servant Naaman, that you may cure him of his leprosy." When the king of Israel read the letter, he tore his clothes and said, "Am I God, to give death or life, that this man sends word to me to cure a man of his leprosy? Just look and see how he is trying to pick a quarrel with me."

But when Elisha the man of God heard that the king of Israel had torn his clothes, he sent a message to the king, "Why have you torn your clothes? Let him come to me, that

he may learn that there is a prophet in Israel." So Naaman
came with his horses and chariots, and halted at the entrance
of Elisha's house. Elisha sent a messenger to him, saying,
"Go, wash in the Jordan seven times, and your flesh shall
be restored and you shall be clean." But Naaman became
angry and went away, saying, "I thought that for me he
would surely come out, and stand and call on the name of
the LORD his God, and would wave his hand over the spot,
and cure the leprosy! Are not Abana and Pharpar, the rivers
of Damascus, better than all the waters of Israel? Could I not
wash in them, and be clean?" He turned and went away in a
rage. But his servants approached and said to him, "Father,
if the prophet had commanded you to do something difficult,
would you not have done it? How much more, when all he
said to you was, 'Wash, and be clean'?" So he went down
and immersed himself seven times in the Jordan, according to
the word of the man of God; his flesh was restored like the
flesh of a young boy, and he was clean.

—2 Kings 5:1–14

In this story, Naaman, a man of much influence, has
a specific idea in mind for how the great prophet of
Israel will heal him of his leprosy. He'll wave hands
dramatically over Naaman's skin, and the disease will
be gone as if by magic. But Elisha doesn't even go
out to meet this important guest; he merely sends a

servant to tell Naaman he needs to dip himself in the Jordan River seven times.

If you have seen the Jordan River, you know that, basically, it's a stream, and in many places it's muddy and uninspiring. Naaman is so insulted at this plan of action that he decides to leave and go home, with his leprosy unhealed. But his servant challenges him to swallow his pride and do as the prophet has instructed. Naaman does relent, dips in the Jordan seven times, and is healed.

More often than we realize, we have notions about exactly how God should help us. We become slaves of our own ideas or slaves of popular opinion or slaves of prestige. Like Naaman, we want the whole show; we want God to heal and help us, but even more, we want God to show how special we are.

When we are truly free—of opinion and preference, of our own ideas—we are then in a position to be healed, however God chooses to do so. When we stop telling God how to help us, we finally can be helped.

What are your thoughts, feelings, and impressions on this topic of receiving? Write in a journal, draw pictures, sing, or move physically if that will help your process.

_____

_____

_____

_____

_____

_____

_____

_____

_____

_____

_____

_____

_____

_____

_____

_____

_____

_____

_____

_____

_____

Use Your Imagination

✝

Bless the LORD, O my soul, and all that is within me, bless
      his holy name.

Bless the LORD, O my soul, and do not forget all his
      benefits—

who forgives all your iniquity, who heals all your diseases,

who redeems your life from the Pit, who crowns you with
      steadfast love and mercy,

who satisfies you with good as long as you live so that your
      youth is renewed like the eagle's.

The LORD works vindication and justice for all who are
      oppressed.

He made known his ways to Moses, his acts to the people
      of Israel.

The LORD is merciful and gracious, slow to anger and
      abounding in steadfast love.

He will not always accuse, nor will he keep his anger
      forever.

He does not deal with us according to our sins, nor repay
      us according to our iniquities.

For as the heavens are high above the earth, so great is his
      steadfast love toward those who fear him;

as far as the east is from the west, so far he removes our
      transgressions from us.

As a father has compassion for his children, so the LORD has
    compassion for those who fear him.
For he knows how we were made; he remembers that we
    are dust.
As for mortals, their days are like grass; they flourish like a
    flower of the field;
for the wind passes over it, and it is gone, and its place
    knows it no more.
But the steadfast love of the LORD is from everlasting to
    everlasting on those who fear him, and his
  righteousness to children's children,
to those who keep his covenant and remember to do his
    commandments.

                        —Psalm 103:1–18

*Try rewriting this psalm in your own words. Imagine
yourself as the recipient of all the graces named here.
Replace any pronouns with "I" and "me" and notice how
that feels.*

_____

_____

_____

_____

_____

_____

_____

_____

_____

_____

_____

_____

_____

_____

Practice Your Freedom

Make a list of the ways in which you need to be healed or helped.

Each day this week, choose one of those needs and journal about it. Think over why it's difficult for you to trust God for that healing. Or explore any ideas or memories or emotions that get in your way of trusting God to help you.

Pray for what you need.

Make some notes here about the action you plan to take this week.

Do the Prayer

✝

After Jesus had finished all his sayings in the hearing of the people, he entered Capernaum. A centurion there had a slave whom he valued highly, and who was ill and close to death. When he heard about Jesus, he sent some Jewish elders to him, asking him to come and heal his slave. When they came to Jesus, they appealed to him earnestly, saying, "He is worthy of having you do this for him, for he loves our people, and it is he who built our synagogue for us." And Jesus went with them, but when he was not far from the house, the centurion sent friends to say to him, "Lord, do not trouble yourself, for I am not worthy to have you come under my roof; therefore I did not presume to come to you. But only speak the word, and let my servant be healed. For I also am a man set under authority, with soldiers under me; and I say to one, 'Go,' and he goes, and to another, 'Come,' and he comes, and to my slave, 'Do this,' and the slave does it." When Jesus heard this he was amazed at him, and turning to the crowd that followed him, he said, "I tell you, not even in Israel have I found such faith." When those who had been sent returned to the house, they found the slave in good health.

—Luke 7:1–10

There were many reasons the centurion might have stayed away and never asked Jesus for help. He was not Jewish; in fact, he was a member of the occupying forces and hated by Jews because of it. For all we know, this man had helped crucify Jews and had participated in brutal actions against people, maybe even against members of Jesus' extended family. He had respect for the Jewish faith—enough to help them build a synagogue—but probably he had never practiced faith for himself, at least not in the Jewish form. Also, his servant was sick, but he was just a servant of the military and of no special importance. People died all the time—why should the centurion expect Jesus to make an effort on his account?

But the centurion did not allow the situation, the politics, his position, his former deeds, or his lack of religious background to get in the way. Perhaps because of his military background, he was free to seek the best solution at hand. He referred to himself as a commander to explain why he believed Jesus need only say the word. This centurion not only approached Jesus despite the differences between them, but he also allowed his specific training as an officer to inform his faith.

Today, there are issues that threaten your freedom with God. You have no faith background—or you have a faith background that was detrimental, even toxic. You come from a family of self-made people who didn't teach you to ask for help. You've done a lot of things you're not proud of. You've never been too good at prayer.

What stands in the way of your walking up to Jesus and asking for what you need? Identify it, and then push it aside and ask. Ask with confidence. Don't hesitate to hope that Jesus will say the word and heal you.

_____

_____

_____

_____

_____

_____

_____

_____

_____

_____

_____

_____

_____

_____

_____

_____

_____

_____

_____

_____

_____

_____

_____

_____

6

Freedom Leads to Contentment

God, my shepherd!
I don't need a thing.
You have bedded me down in lush meadows,
you find me quiet pools to drink from.
True to your word,
you let me catch my breath
and send me in the right direction.

Even when the way goes through
Death Valley,
I'm not afraid
when you walk at my side.
Your trusty shepherd's crook
makes me feel secure.

You serve me a six-course dinner
    right in front of my enemies.
You revive my drooping head;
my cup brims with blessing.

Your beauty and love chase after me
    every day of my life.
I'm back home in the house of God
    for the rest of my life.

—Psalm 23, *The Message*

Here's the Idea: We Are Free When We Rest in God's Care

✝

Not that I am referring to being in need; for I have learned to be content with whatever I have. I know what it is to have little, and I know what it is to have plenty. In any and all circumstances I have learned the secret of being well-fed and of going hungry, of having plenty and of being in need. I can do all things through him who strengthens me.

—Philippians 4:11–13

Ignatian spirituality encourages an attitude of indifference. This doesn't mean we have ceased to care but that we have stopped pushing toward a specific outcome. When we live by faith in a loving God, we are free to adjust to an ever-changing situation. Perhaps we really want this job, but we say to God, "I do want this job. But I know that you see beyond this job and this moment. I know that my life will be abundant even if I don't get the job."

This attitude can extend to all areas of life: where we live, which house or apartment we buy (or rent), where we go to school, how we resolve health problems, whom we choose in relationships, and so on. We love the romantic notion that we have found "the one" person to be our lifelong partner, but if we don't hold that relationship gently, we can cripple it. Most of us have experienced feeling pushed and pulled, or doing that to someone else. What if this person doesn't love you in return? Even in an area as critical as love relationships, indifference can free both people to act from their own volition, to offer love rather than have it demanded.

St. Ignatius spoke of getting to the point that he would not desire riches over poverty or good health over poor health. He wasn't trying to tear down his life or compromise its quality; he was merely expressing complete faith in God's love and in its ability to transcend every situation.

What are your thoughts, feelings, and impressions on this topic of contentment? Write in a journal, draw pictures, sing, or move physically if that will help your process.

_____

_____

_____

_____

_____

_____

_____

_____

_____

_____

_____

_____

_____

Use Your Imagination

✝

When Jesus saw the crowds, he went up the mountain; and after he sat down, his disciples came to him. Then he began to speak, and taught them, saying:

"Blessed are the poor in spirit, for theirs is the kingdom of heaven.

"Blessed are those who mourn, for they will be comforted.

"Blessed are the meek, for they will inherit the earth.

"Blessed are those who hunger and thirst for righteousness, for they will be filled.

"Blessed are the merciful, for they will receive mercy.

"Blessed are the pure in heart, for they will see God.

"Blessed are the peacemakers, for they will be called children of God.

"Blessed are those who are persecuted for righteousness' sake, for theirs is the kingdom of heaven.

"Blessed are you when people revile you and persecute you and utter all kinds of evil against you falsely on my account. Rejoice and be glad, for your reward is great in heaven, for in the same way they persecuted the prophets who were before you.

—Matthew 5:1–11

You find yourself in a large public park with a few trees, an old fountain, and some broken playground equipment. The grass is burnt from the summer heat. Once, this was a beautiful place—now, not so much. Yet there are at least five hundred people gathered near one of the more substantial shade trees. Under the tree stands the teacher. Why he's here, in this inner-city park rather than at one of the fancy hotels downtown, you can't even guess. But he's here, and there's no price for admission. So you stand in the heat, pressed into the huddle of people, all straining to hear every word.

Then he starts telling you—and everyone else—how blessed you are. He describes the various situations represented in the crowd: poverty, frustration, hunger, grief, anger at injustice, desire to resolve complex conflicts, and longing for what will bring the community peace and enjoyment. You expected him to talk about heaven and to offer hope by pointing to some distant, wonderful place and time. But no. He isn't speaking hypothetically at all. He is describing *your* life, *right now*. And he's pronouncing it blessed by God.

After a while, the teacher finishes talking. You go up and shake his hand, thanking him for his words. He clasps your hand in his and makes certain to meet your gaze. He smiles and says again, "God blesses you. Bless you."

Then you go home. You look around at your life. You see in detail the place where you live, the people who appear regularly in your days. You see the job you have—or you remember the job you lost. You spend time watching members of your family deal with their stresses, and you listen to their conversations.

God blesses you. God blesses this.

Which lines of the Beatitudes, in these words of Jesus, apply to you right now? How are you blessed?

_____

_____

_____

_____

_____

_____

_____

_____

_____

_____

_____

_____

_____

Practice Your Freedom

Celebrate your life this week. Be systematic if that helps, choosing a different focus each day.

- Choose to be content with your physical home one day.

- Choose to be grateful for employment another day.

- Celebrate how passionate you still become when you see others treated hatefully and unjustly.

- Enjoy the deep longing you have for forests and streams to be unpolluted and for crops to be grown for optimum health rather than for mere profit.

- Thank God for the "stimulating" discussions you've had lately about the need for moral financial management or for humane treatment of people who are homeless.

Choose contentment. Look at your life and see it as blessed.

*Make some notes here about the action you plan to take
this week.*

_____

_____

_____

_____

_____

_____

_____

_____

_____

_____

_____

_____

_____

_____

_____

_____

_____

_____

_____

_____

_____

_____

_____

Do the Prayer

✝

Though the fig tree does not blossom,
　　and no fruit is on the vines;
though the produce of the olive fails
　　and the fields yield no food;
though the flock is cut off from the fold
　　and there is no herd in the stalls,
yet I will rejoice in the LORD;
　　I will exult in the God of my salvation.

—Habakkuk 3:17–18

The prophet describes a situation that, in the ancient East, would have been devastating: massive crop failure. He has seen people starving; he has watched the land die a slow death. Yet he makes this incredible statement—"No matter what happens, I will celebrate the God of my salvation."

You probably do not live in an economy that depends on a good fig or olive crop. So rewrite the words of Habakkuk to reflect *your* reality. You are writing a prayer that says, in essence, "Even if [blank] doesn't happen, I will rejoice."

_____

_____

_____

_____

_____

_____

_____

_____

_____

_____

_____

_____

_____

Moving On . . .

First of all, consider that you've done significant work with the material in this book. One or two chapters may stand out as being particularly meaningful. Some parts probably worked better than others. In one chapter, you might have related well to the idea, but the prayer didn't flow. Or in another case, the prayer seemed to ring in your depths, but the imaginative work fell flat. There's nothing wrong with this uneven kind of reaction to the meditations. Don't worry about what didn't "work." What you want to pay attention to is the different kinds of interior movements you experienced. Concentrate on what tugged at you—whether the tug was positive or negative. Sometimes the negative tugs are also necessary and point us to what needs our attention.

Go back over your journal notes. Look for clues about what's happening in your soul in this area we call freedom.

- Write down some statements that describe what you understand about freedom.

- Write down some questions you still have about how freedom works on a day-to-day basis.

- Write down several statements of gratitude about specific moments, prayers, or revelations that have helped you.

If you are able, have four conversations about the work you've done. Have one conversation with God your Creator (or, if you prefer, God as father or mother). Have another conversation with Jesus, your teacher and companion. Have a conversation with Mary or another saint, or with the Holy Spirit, who is your helper in prayer. Finally, have a conversation with a living person you know and feel at liberty to include in this spiritual process.

About the Author

Vinita Hampton Wright is a Loyola Press editor and writer of many books, including *Days of Deepening Friendship* and *Simple Acts of Moving Forward*, and she blogs for DeepeningFriendship.com. She has been practicing Ignatian spirituality for a decade and writing about it for nearly as long. She lives in Chicago, IL, with her husband, two dogs, and two cats.